W9-CFK-983

WEEKLY **WR** READER®
EARLY LEARNING LIBRARY

Where on Earth? World Geography

Mountains

by JoAnn Early Macken

Reading consultant: Susan Nations, M.Ed.,
author, literacy coach,
and consultant in literacy development

Learning from Maps

You can learn many things from maps if you know how to read them. This page will help you understand how to read a map.

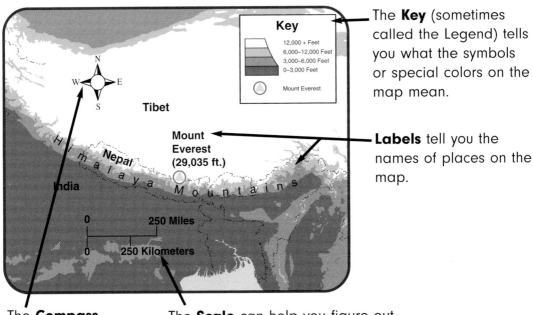

Key

12,000 + Feet
6,000–12,000 Feet
3,000–6,000 Feet
0–3,000 Feet

Mount Everest

N
W—E
S

Tibet

Himalaya

Nepal

India

Mount
Everest
(29,035 ft.)

Mountains

0   250 Miles

0   250 Kilometers

The **Key** (sometimes called the Legend) tells you what the symbols or special colors on the map mean.

Labels tell you the names of places on the map.

The **Compass Rose** tells you which way is North, South, East, and West.

The **Scale** can help you figure out how big or far apart places on the map are. For example, a distance of 1 inch (2.5 centimeters) on a map may be hundreds of miles in the real world.

Table of Contents

What Is a Mountain? 4

How Do Mountains Form? 6

Changing Mountains......................12

Life on a Mountain 15

People and Mountains 18

Spotlight: Mount Everest..................21

Glossary 22

For More Information......................23

Index 24

Cover and title page: Mount Rainier has snow and ice at its top all year. It is located near Seattle, Washington.

These mountains are part of the Alps. The Alps are a range of mountains in Europe.

What Is a Mountain?

A mountain is a huge pile of rock and earth. Some mountains are so high they reach into the clouds. Their **peaks**, or tops, may be snowy all year. Other mountains are low enough to climb in one day. Most mountains are linked to others in long chains. The chains are called **ranges**.

Young mountains have sharp edges. Older mountains have smooth edges and rounded peaks. They have been worn down by the weather over many years. All mountains take millions of years to form.

Many mountains have high, rocky peaks.

How Do Mountains Form?

Mountains are found all over the world. They are even found in oceans. Some mountains rise above an ocean's surface, creating islands.

Earth's outside layer is called the **crust**. It is made up of sections called **plates**. Below the crust is a layer of hot, partly melted rock. The plates move slowly on the liquid rock. Where plates meet, mountains may form. The hot, liquid rock creates mountains, too.

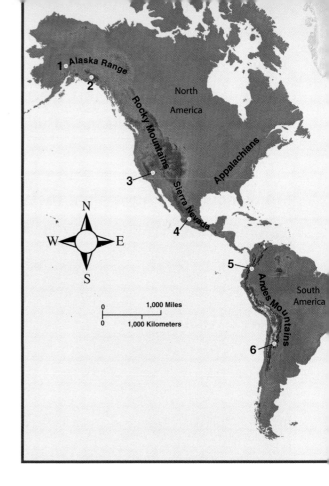

This map shows major mountain ranges and the tallest mountains in the world.

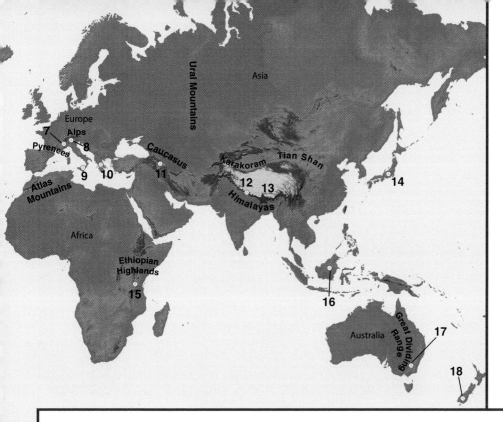

Key   ★ = World's Tallest Mountain   ⬤ = Famous Mountain

1. McKinley 20,323 ft (6,194 m)
2. Logan 19,850 ft (6,050 m)
3. Whitney 14,495 ft (4,418 m)
4. Popocatépetl 17,888 ft (5,542 m)
5. Cotopaxi 19,348 ft (5,897 m)
6. Aconcagua 22,836 ft (6,960 m)
7. Mont Blanc 15,772 ft (4,807 m)
8. Matterhorn 14,692 ft (4,478 m)
9. Etna 10,902 ft (3,323m)

10. Olympus 9,550 ft (2,911 m)
11. Ararat 16,946 ft (5,165 m)
12. K2 28,253 ft (8,611 m)
13. Everest 29,035 ft (8,850 m)
14. Fuji 12,388 ft (3,776 m)
15. Kilimanjaro 19,341 ft (5,895 m)
16. Kinabalu 13,432 ft (4,094 m)
17. Kosciuszko 7,310 ft (2,228 m)
18. Cook 12,350 ft (3,764 m)

Mount Everest is the tallest mountain in the world.

These red rocks in Sedona, Arizona, have many layers.

The plates in Earth's crust bump into each other. One plate may slide under another plate. Near the surface of Earth, layers of rock get pushed together. They crack and fold. They lift up. The folded layers of rock create a mountain.

Mountains also form in places where plates move apart and hot melted rock rises up. When the rock cools and hardens, it can form mountains.

A break in a layer of rocks is a **fault**. A fault can be a huge crack in the crust. The rocks on the two sides of the fault can slide past each other. One side can rise, and the other can drop. The higher side can form a mountain.

This cliff in California shows a fault in a layer of rock.

Hot lava flows from a volcano. When the lava cools, it will be hard rock.

Some mountains are volcanos. Molten rock, or **magma**, pours up through cracks in Earth's crust. When it flows out of a volcano, the magma is known as **lava**. Lava hardens into rock as it cools. Lava can flow out of a volcano over and over. Each lava flow adds a layer of rock to the mountain.

Magma can push up from under the crust. It can form a dome like a bubble. Then the magma can harden under the crust. This dome is another kind of mountain.

Pikes Peak is in Colorado. It is a dome mountain. It was formed when magma pushed upward beneath Earth's crust.

These mountains are in New Hampshire. They are slowly changing over time.

Changing Mountains

Air is colder higher up. Cold air freezes rocks. They warm up in the Sun and cool down at night. Rocks can freeze and thaw over and over again. Over time, they crack. Pieces can break off and fall away.

Wind wears away the soil. Wind carries bits of sand and stone that grind down the rock.

Ice and snow loosen pieces of rock. Water pulls the rocks away. They scrape against other rocks in the mountain and wear them down.

Glaciers also **carve**, or cut, away soil. They carry rocks that dig into the land. Mountains are always wearing down.

Glaciers are rivers of ice. As they move, glaciers can wear down mountains.

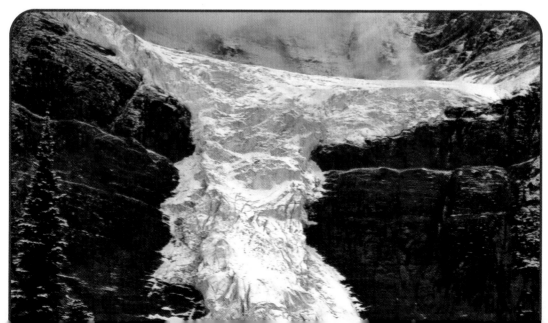

During a rock slide, huge amounts of rock may fall.

A storm or an earthquake can loosen a whole hillside.
It can fall away in a huge rock slide.

In winter, mountains get thick layers of snow. New
snow, a warm wind, or warmer temperatures can loosen
the layers of snow. One layer may start to slide. As it
moves, it gathers more snow and gains speed. This
falling snow is called an **avalanche**.

Life on a Mountain

On mountains, water can be hard to find. Mountains may have a rainy, wet side and a dry side. Even on the wet side, water will run off. Wind dries the water quickly.

Many plants grow close to the ground or in cracks. There, they can soak up any water that appears. Trees cannot grow above a certain height on the mountain, called the **tree line**. At the top of tall peaks, no plants can grow.

No plants grow at the top of this mountain.

A pika is a small mountain animal that is related to rabbits.

Birds of all sizes nest in the mountains. They eat seeds, plants, and insects.

Small animals eat mountain plants. Some of them **hibernate**, or sleep, through the winter.

Mountain goats have long, shaggy coats. They leap from boulder to boulder. Wolves make their dens away from the wind. They hunt for elk and other animals.

Llamas and yaks also live in high places. Cougars, bobcats, and lynxes all find food in mountain areas.

Gorillas, monkeys, and leopards live on African slopes.

These llamas live in the Andes mountain range of South America.

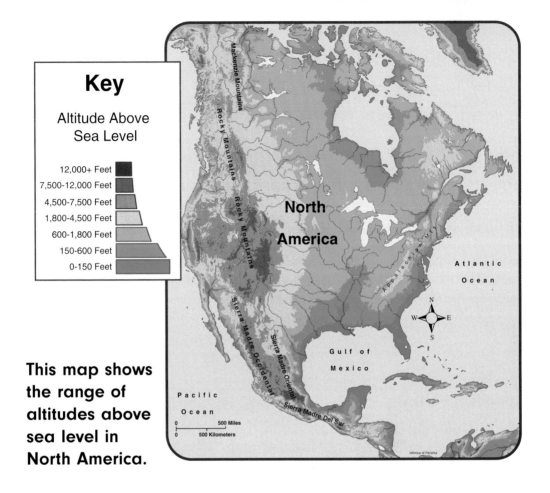

Key

Altitude Above Sea Level

12,000+ Feet	
7,500-12,000 Feet	
4,500-7,500 Feet	
1,800-4,500 Feet	
600-1,800 Feet	
150-600 Feet	
0-150 Feet	

This map shows the range of altitudes above sea level in North America.

People and Mountains

Mountains are home to many people. Some people like to climb mountains or ski down them. Others love mountains for their wide views of the land below.

Gold, silver, coal, copper, and iron are found in many mountains. Some people **mine**, or dig, for them. In some places, people have farms on mountains. They build terraces, which look like steps. Sometimes, the terraces have stone walls. The walls keep the soil from washing away.

People farm on this mountain. Crops grow on each terrace.

A dog herds sheep on a hillside in Idaho.

In some places, people bring cattle and sheep up to mountains in spring. The animals eat grass there until fall. Then, they come back down to lower fields. They stay in warmer places during the winter.

Spotlight: Mount Everest

Mount Everest is the world's highest mountain. It rises more than 5 miles (8 kilometers) above sea level. Mt. Everest is part of the Himalaya mountain range. It is in Asia, on the border between the country of Nepal and Tibet, which is part of China.

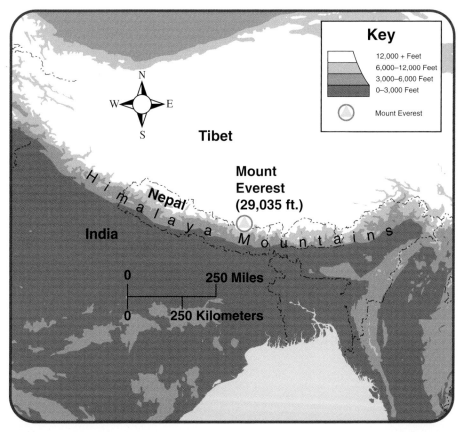

Key

12,000 + Feet
6,000–12,000 Feet
3,000–6,000 Feet
0–3,000 Feet

Mount Everest

Tibet

Mount Everest (29,035 ft.)

Himalaya Mountains

Nepal

India

0 — 250 Miles

0 — 250 Kilometers

This map shows the height of Mount Everest and areas around it.

Glossary

dome — a rounded top or roof

glaciers — large rivers of ice that usually move very slowly

grind — to rub, pound, or crush something into very small pieces or powder

hibernate — to spend the winter in an inactive state, such as sleeping or resting

molten rock — melted rock that is formed below the surface of Earth

terraces — series of flat areas of earth rising one above the other

thaw — to warm up after being frozen; to melt

volcanoes — holes in Earth's crust where lava, rocks, and ashes flow from inside Earth

For More Information

Books

The Appalachians. Charles W. Maynard (PowerKids Press)

Bighorn Sheep. Animals That Live in the Mountains (series). JoAnn Early Macken (Weekly Reader Early Learning Library).

I Live in the Mountains. Where I Live (series). Gini Holland (Weekly Reader Early Learning Library)

Living in the Mountains. Allan Fowler (Children's Press)

Mountains. Andy Owen and Miranda Ashwell (Heinemann)

Mountains. Anna O'Mara (Bridgestone)

Web Sites

Denali for Kids
www.pbs.org/wgbh/nova/denali/kids
Survival skills, maps, and tips from experts about Mount Denali

Volcano World Virtual Field Trips
volcano.und.edu/vwdocs/kids/vrtrips.html
Pictures from Mount St. Helens, Hawaii, and Mars

Index

animals 16, 17, 20
crust 6, 8, 9, 10, 11
faults 9
glaciers 13
islands 6
lava 10
magma 10, 11

Mount Everest 6, 7, 21
peaks 4, 5, 15
people 18, 19, 20
plants 15, 16
plates 6, 8, 9
rocks 4, 6, 8, 9, 10, 12, 13, 14

snow 3, 4, 13, 14
terraces 19
weather 5, 14
wind 12, 14, 15, 17

About the Author

JoAnn Early Macken is the author of two rhyming picture books, *Sing-Along Song* and *Cats on Judy*, and more than eighty nonfiction books for children. Her poems have appeared in several children's magazines. A graduate of the M.F.A. in Writing for Children and Young Adults Program at Vermont College, she lives in Wisconsin with her husband and their two sons.

Please visit our web site at: **www.earlyliteracy.cc**
For a free color catalog describing **Weekly Reader**®
Early Learning Library's list of high-quality books,
call 1-877-445-5824 (USA) or 1-800-387-3178 (Canada).
Weekly Reader® Early Learning Library's fax: (414) 336-0164.

Library of Congress Cataloging-in-Publication Data

Macken, JoAnn Early, 1953–
  Mountains / JoAnn Early Macken.
    p. cm. — (Where on earth? world geography)
  Includes bibliographical references and index.
  ISBN 0-8368-6395-X (lib. bdg.)
  ISBN 0-8368-6402-6 (softcover)
  1. Mountains—Juvenile literature. I. Title.
  GB512.M32   2006
  551.43—dc22   2005025576

This edition first published in 2006 by
Weekly Reader® Early Learning Library
A Member of the WRC Media Family of Companies
330 West Olive Street, Suite 100
Milwaukee, WI 53212 USA

Copyright © 2006 by Weekly Reader® Early Learning Library

Editors: Jim Mezzanotte and Barbara Kiely Miller
Art direction: Tammy West
Cover design and page layout: Kami Strunsee
Picture research: Diane Laska-Swanke

Picture credits: Cover, title, pp. 4, 12, 17 © James P. Rowan; pp. 2, 6-7,
18, 21 Kami Strunsee/© Weekly Reader Early Learning Library, 2006; pp. 5,
13, 15, 16 © Tom and Pat Leeson; p. 8 © Deborah Long/Visuals Unlimited;
pp. 9, 14 © Marli Miller/Visuals Unlimited; p. 10 © Bruce Davidson/
naturepl.com; p. 11 © Doug Sokell/Visuals Unlimited; p. 19 © David
Cavagnaro/Visuals Unlimited; p. 20 © Paul Dix/Visuals Unlimited

Printed in the United States of America

1 2 3 4 5 6 7 8 9 10 09 08 07 06